Richard Nixon

History Maker Bios

Madeline Donaldson

BARNES & NOBLE

NEW YORK

Illustrations by Tad Butler

ISBN-13: 978-1-4351-0167-8
ISBN-10: 1-4351-0167-7

Printed and bound in the United States of America

1 3 5 7 9 10 8 6 4 2

TABLE OF CONTENTS

INTRODUCTION

On August 9, 1974, U.S. president Richard Nixon waved his arms broadly at the crowd. He was about to board a helicopter. It would take him to Air Force One, the president's plane. Was Richard Nixon off to a foreign country? Was he meeting a world leader? Was he traveling to give an important speech?

No. President Nixon had just quit his job. Government leaders had determined he had gone against the U.S. Constitution. Americans viewed him as dishonest. This wasn't the first time the people's opinion of Richard Nixon had dropped low. But he had once enjoyed great popularity. Richard Nixon had become used to the ups and downs of politics. He believed someday he'd be on the upswing again.

This is his story.

1 Boys, Boys Boys

Frank and Hannah Nixon had a lot of boys—five in all. Dick was the second son. His formal name was Richard Milhous Nixon. He was born on January 9, 1913. Hannah named him after the English king Richard the Lion-Hearted. Milhous was her last name before she married Frank.

Hannah belonged to a family of religious thinkers called Quakers. Frank had become a Quaker after marrying Hannah.

WHO ARE THE QUAKERS?

The Quakers, also called the Society of Friends, are a religious group. The group started in the mid-1600s in England. The Friends disagreed with the Church of England, that country's national religion. The government charged them with breaking English laws. Many Quakers went to prison for their beliefs. The Quakers kept meeting anyway.

Eventually, a group of Quakers left England for the English colony of Pennsylvania. They hoped they could practice their religion freely in North America. Among the new arrivals were Thomas and Sarah Milhous. They were Richard Nixon's ancestors on his mother's side.

Dick already had an older brother named Harold. Soon, Donald and Arthur came along. Much later, Edward was born. Over the years, the Nixons lived in several small towns in Southern California. Dick was born in the house Frank built in Yorba Linda. Frank was trying to set up a lemon grove there. But the trees weren't doing well.

Dick was born in this house in Yorba Linda, California. His father, Frank, built the house in the early 1910s.

This family portrait is from 1917. Dick is standing on the right.

Dick was quiet and serious, like his mother. Hannah was well educated and came from a well–to–do family in nearby Whittier. Dick's nearest brothers, Harold and Don, were outgoing, like their father. Frank said what he thought and enjoyed a good argument. He had a quick temper. Although they were very different, Dick's parents had a true fondness for each other. They taught their children the value of hard work and of never giving up.

Dick (CENTER WITH CAP) and his brothers pose for a picture in the early 1920s.

Dick was close to his baby brother Arthur, who was born in 1918. He took him for walks. He noted the changes as Arthur grew from a tiny baby into a toddler. The next year, when Dick was six, the lemon grove failed. Family life became hard. In 1920, Hannah started packing lemons for a fruit company. At the same time, Dick and Don picked string beans on farms. Nixon would later say, "I still hate the sight of string beans."

Meanwhile, Dick started elementary school. Hannah had already taught him how to read. He had a talent for memorizing information. He could recite long passages of text. His teachers noted his keen mind. They allowed him to skip grades.

In 1922, when Dick was nine, the family moved to Whittier. The Nixons set up a gas station and then added a grocery store. Everyone in the family worked to make the business a success. Every morning, Hannah got up early to bake pies to sell. Frank spent long hours at the store. The boys helped with chores.

Frank Nixon's service station was a family business. Dick helped with chores.

Even with all the work, Dick continued to do well in school. He especially liked to debate. In these contests, participants argue according to rules. He seemed driven to get good grades to please his parents. Then sadness struck the family. Arthur became sick. He had headaches and stomachaches. He couldn't eat. He died of a brain disease in August 1925. Dick was heartbroken.

After Arthur died, Dick was even more driven to succeed. He graduated first in his class in 1926. Then he went on to high school. He got nearly perfect grades in

English, Latin, math, and science. He also joined the football squad. But Dick knew he wasn't good at the game.

This photograph from 1927 shows Dick with his violin.

He played violin in the school orchestra and was on the debating team. He worked to perfect his debating style. But still, classmates saw Dick as a loner. He was shy and ill at ease, especially with girls.

Another family tragedy struck in 1927. Doctors told the Nixons that Harold had a lung disease called tuberculosis. To improve Harold's health, Hannah moved him to the dry air in Arizona. Sometimes, in the summer, Dick visited Harold. To pay for these trips, Dick worked at various jobs in Arizona. But he returned to California to go back to school.

2 WORK, SCHOOL, MARRIAGE, AND THE NAVY

By 1928, Dick was in charge of buying and displaying fruits and vegetables at the store. He got up early before school to get everything done. He was still an excellent student, with a strong drive to succeed. He gave up football and orchestra to work. But he stayed on the debate team. In 1930, he graduated third in his class.

Dick thought he'd like to go to a college on the East Coast. But bills for Harold's care squashed that idea. In addition, seventeen–year–old Dick got another brother in 1930, when Edward was born. So Dick enrolled at local Whittier College. He tested his leadership skills by winning the freshman class presidency. He took part in football, basketball, and track. But he wasn't good at any of these sports. He did well, however, in the debating society. The Whittier team won many local contests.

Dick (CENTER) played on the Whittier College football team. His true talent, however, was in debate.

THE ORTHOGONIANS

While at Whittier College, Dick helped start a men's club. The college already had the Franklins. The members of this group were mostly from rich families. Dick and his classmates wanted something for people who came from more modest backgrounds. They formed the Orthogonians. The name stands for "on-the-square." Dick became the society's first president and wrote the society's constitution.

Even though Whittier College was small, it had some bright students. Dick had to work hard to compete. He often studied late into the night. Dick was already planning to become a lawyer. In 1933, he campaigned to become student body president. He won, but that same year, Harold died. Still, Dick pressed on and graduated second in his class in 1934.

The Nixon store was doing well. But the family still didn't have the money to send Dick to law school. With his strong grades, he won a scholarship to Duke University in Durham, North Carolina. He again worked hard to keep up his grades. His good memory also helped. The law school courses were built around remembering legal cases. Dick was outstanding at this part of the work.

This portrait was taken during Dick's freshman year at Duke Law School.

But he was still not sure he was up to the challenge of competing against students from better schools. Although he pushed himself to succeed, he lacked self-confidence. Friends saw him as hard working but humorless and lonely. They nicknamed him Gloomy Gus. Yet no one saw Dick's inner passion to do well, to win at all costs. In 1936, he became president of Duke's law school student group. He graduated third in his class the next year.

Dick (BACK ROW, FAR RIGHT) sits with his classmates, the Duke University Law School class of 1937.

Dick expected good job offers after graduation. But the United States was still going through the Depression. Good jobs were hard to find. He went back to Whittier and got a job with a local law firm. For four years, he worked on legal cases. He still lived with his parents and worked at the store.

Meanwhile, Dick got involved with local business and civic groups. He joined the Chamber of Commerce and the Kiwanis Club. He became a member of the Republican Party. Being part of these groups taught Dick about local centers of power. He began to think about winning local public office as a future goal.

Dick became a partner two years after starting to practice law. Here he stands at the door of his law office.

He also acted with the Community Players, Whittier's theater group. There he met Patricia Ryan. Her style and self-confidence struck him from the first meeting. He knew right away that he wanted to marry her. And he even told her so! Pat didn't take him seriously. Dick tried to win her for two years. He wrote her long letters and even some poems. Finally, she agreed. They married in June 1940.

Dick wanted to get on with his career. Staying in Whittier didn't fit his goals.

Dick married Patricia Ryan in Riverside, California, on June 21, 1940.

At this time, countries in Europe and Asia were fighting World War II (1939–1945). On December 7, 1941, the Japanese attacked Pearl Harbor, a base in Hawaii. The United States entered the war. That same year, the U.S. government formed the Office of Price Administration (OPA) in Washington, D.C. The OPA controlled prices. It also oversaw how much people could buy of certain products during wartime. The OPA was looking for young lawyers to staff the agency. Friends from Duke recommended Dick. Pat was all for the move. And Dick saw the job as a way to further his political goals. But soon, he grew bored with the paperwork.

Dick enlisted in the U.S. Navy in 1942. After months of officer training, he shipped out to the South Pacific in May 1943. He served with the South Pacific Combat Air Transport Command (SCAT). His job was to make sure supplies got from cargo planes to the war zones. SCAT also helped wounded soldiers get on planes to go home.

Dick (RIGHT) served in the U.S. Navy in the South Pacific during World War II.

Dick was never in the thick of fighting. But his work helped pilots, soldiers, and marines. In July 1944, he returned to the United States. He was able to leave the navy in late 1945.

3 POLITICAL PROGRESS

In October 1945, a Republican friend in Whittier asked Dick Nixon if he'd run for the U.S. Congress in California's Twelfth District. Nixon quickly agreed. He faced Jerry Voorhis, the Democrat who held the seat. At this time, Americans were afraid that Communists would take over the United States. Nixon and his supporters said Voorhis was a Communist. There was no proof of this. But their scare tactic worked. Nixon won the race with 57 percent of the vote.

Pat didn't like how mean the campaign was. She mainly stayed in the background. But she and Nixon rejoiced at the birth of their daughter Tricia in February 1946. (Another daughter, Julie, was born in 1948.)

As a congressman, Nixon served on the House Un-American Activities Committee (HUAC). This committee tried to find Communist spies. In 1948, it took up the cause of Whittaker Chambers. He was a former Communist spy for the Soviet Union. (This country was made up of fifteen republics, including Russia, in Eastern

Europe and northern Asia.) He said Alger Hiss was also a Communist spy. Hiss had been an important presidential adviser. Hiss denied the charges.

Nixon holds his newborn daughter Tricia in 1946.

Anti-Communism

After World War II, the United States and the Soviet Union became bitter enemies. The two countries had very different kinds of governments. The United States has a capitalist system. Under this system, people can own their own property and businesses. The Soviet Union had a Communist system. The Soviet government owned all property and businesses. The two countries competed for power. Each wanted to control and influence other nations. During Nixon's early career, being against Communism was a popular stand. Part of Nixon's early success was tied to his efforts to prove that Alger Hiss was a Communist spy.

Nixon urged the HUAC to keep looking into the matter. Eventually, a U.S. court found Hiss guilty of lying to the HUAC. The court sentenced him to five years in prison.

The Hiss case made Nixon famous. In 1949, the Republican Party asked him to run for the U.S. Senate. He faced the Democratic candidate, Helen Gahagan Douglas. Nixon and his supporters again ran a negative campaign. They tricked voters into believing Douglas was friendly to Communists. The scare tactic worked again. Nixon won by a large margin.

In 1951, the Republican Party picked  Dwight Eisenhower to be its candidate for president. He chose Nixon to be the vice-presidential candidate. But before the appointment was final, trouble sprang up.

Nixon campaigns for the U.S. Senate from the tailgate of his car in 1950.

Dwight Eisenhower (LEFT) picked Nixon to be his running mate for the 1952 presidential election.

Newspapers said Nixon wrongly used money donated by supporters. They said he used the money for his personal expenses, when it was for his campaign. Nixon denied the charges. But advisers told Eisenhower to find another running mate. With Pat at his side, Nixon made a speech on TV. He said the fund paid for political work beyond his Senate duties. The speech helped make viewers believe him. Eisenhower kept Nixon as his vice-presidential choice. They won the election in 1952 and again in 1956.

Nixon was an active vice president.
He traveled to Asia, Europe, and South
America. He also stepped in for Eisenhower
when the president was ill for a time in
1955, 1956, and 1957. By 1960, Nixon had
become the Republican Party's choice
to run for president. His Democratic
opponent was Senator John Kennedy of
Massachusetts. Neither candidate had a
clear lead during the campaign. On Election
Day, Kennedy narrowly beat Nixon.

*Nixon (RIGHT) debates John F. Kennedy in a televised
debate during the 1960 presidential election.*

Nixon went back to California. He ran against the state's Democratic governor, Pat Brown, in 1962 but lost. After the loss, Nixon declared that he was leaving politics. He also got angry at the media. He felt reporters had treated him unfairly. He said, "You won't have Nixon to kick around any more." But Nixon never really lost his desire to become president. He moved to New York City and became a partner in a big law firm. He tried to keep himself in the public eye. He wrote articles, met with world leaders, and gave speeches. By 1967, he had built up enough support to seek the Republican Party's nomination for president once again.

Nixon waves to the crowd during the 1968 presidential campaign.

MR. PRESIDENT

By the late 1960s, the United States was being torn in many directions. Many people were protesting the U.S. role in the Vietnam War (1957–1975). The murders of two leaders, New York senator Robert Kennedy and Dr. Martin Luther King Jr., shocked the nation. Many large cities reacted with waves of rioting.

During the 1968 presidential campaign, Nixon presented himself as a law-and-order candidate. He said he could stop the rioting and bring the country together. Republicans again chose him to run for president. Nixon came across as a mature man with a lot of national and international experience. He beat the Democratic candidate, Vice President Hubert Humphrey, in another close presidential race.

Nixon takes the oath of office for the presidency at the U.S. Capitol on January 20, 1969.

As president, Nixon first focused on the Vietnam War. Young people were protesting strongly against the war. He organized a way to take U.S. troops out of Vietnam gradually. But he also ordered secret bombing raids. He hoped these bombings would force peace talks to happen.

Nixon had some successes within the United States. He set up the Environmental Protection Agency. Its job was to protect water, air, and land in the United States from pollution. He signed the law that lowered the voting age from twenty–one to eighteen. In 1969, he spoke to *Apollo 11* astronauts as they made their historic landing on the moon. Another bright moment for the Nixon family came in 1971. Tricia married a young lawyer named Edward Cox at the White House.

Nixon walks Tricia down the stairs to the Rose Garden for her wedding.

President and Mrs. Nixon visit the Great Wall of China in 1972.

Meanwhile, Nixon thought about the huge country of China, a strongly Communist nation. Few capitalist countries, such as the United States, had ties with China. Nixon was still as anti–Communist as ever. But he thought the United States should be able to do business with China. In a bold move, he and Pat traveled there in 1972. Only Nixon could balance anti–Communist views and U.S. business needs. After that trip, the United States was open to working with China.

Meanwhile, the Soviet Union was still fiercely competing with the United States. Each country wanted to have the most damaging weapons. Nixon told his staff to talk with Soviet leaders. They discussed ways to stop the weapons competition. The result was the Strategic Arms Limitation Talks (SALT) of 1972. These talks led to an agreement that put some limits on the numbers and kinds of weapons each country had.

Nixon (SITTING ON LEFT) and Russian leader Leonid Brezhnev (SITTING ON RIGHT) sign the SALT treaty in 1972.

But the Nixon government also had some problems. Prices, especially for foreign oil, were rising. Americans were becoming more angry about the Vietnam War. They pushed for change through antiwar protests. Many of the protests turned violent. Some protesters were even killed or injured.

Picketers protesting the Vietnam War gather outside a hotel hosting a Nixon speech.

Nixon saw the 1972 presidential campaign as a battle against the Democrats. He viewed them as his enemies. He was determined to win big.

To do this, he highlighted his international successes. In addition, he ordered his staff to find ways to make the Democratic challengers look bad. Most of these efforts were illegal. For example, he set up secret groups to punish anyone who gave Republican campaign information to the press. At the same time, some of Nixon's advisers arranged for burglars to steal secret information from the Democratic campaign office. Nixon secretly taped talks he had with his own staff. He trusted almost no one. For Nixon, all that mattered was winning. He easily won a second term as president in 1972.

5 WATERGATE AND BEYOND

During the 1972 campaign, a group of Nixon supporters broke into the Watergate office building in Washington, D.C. The Democratic Party had offices there. To the public, the break-in seemed like a prank. That was exactly how Nixon wanted it to look. He and his staff had set up a complex cover–up.

But two young reporters, Bob Woodward and Carl Bernstein, kept digging for more information. The trial of the burglars in early 1973 linked them to highly placed Nixon advisers. The advisers had known about the burglary. In fact, they were paying the burglars to keep quiet. The media got more interested in the Woodward-Bernstein reports. So did the U.S. Congress. It set up committees to look into the cover-up and Nixon's part in it. Members of the White House staff talked to the committees. They said Nixon had known about the cover-up from the very beginning. He had urged lying and other illegal acts to fool the public. Some of the proof was in meetings Nixon had secretly taped.

Carl Bernstein (LEFT) and Robert Woodward uncovered the Watergate scandal.

Within months of his second term, Nixon's presidency was falling apart. The Watergate scandal was almost the only thing people were talking about. One by one, his advisers were convicted of crimes. Each conviction brought wrongdoing closer to Nixon himself. It seemed likely that he would be removed from office.

Impeaching the President

The process of getting rid of a U.S. president—called impeachment—isn't easy. And it's not supposed to be. The U.S. Constitution says the president can be removed by being convicted of treason, bribery, or other serious crimes. Impeachment involves both parts of the U.S. Congress—the House of Representatives and the Senate. The House looks into the charges. If House members vote to impeach, then the Senate puts the case for impeachment on trial.

Nixon speaks to the nation in 1974. Next to him are written copies of the White House tapes.

In 1974, a House committee passed three impeachment articles, or charges, against Richard Nixon. Article I said Nixon's efforts to cover up Watergate had blocked justice. Article II said Nixon had misused his power as president. Article III said he had gone against the Constitution by scorning Congress. This happened when he refused to give White House tapes to Congress. The committee's final report said Nixon should be impeached.

To avoid impeachment, Nixon resigned on August 9, 1974. His vice president, Gerald Ford, took over as president. On September 8, 1974, Ford pardoned Nixon of any crimes he may have committed. Ford thought the pardon would help the nation put Watergate behind it and move on.

After the resignation, the Nixons went to their house in San Clemente, California. Pat was happy to live a quiet life. But Nixon didn't want Watergate to define his presidency. He wanted to be known for something more than lying and covering up crimes. He first tackled writing his life story. Published in 1978, the book was well received by the public.

In 1980, he and Pat moved to the East Coast. Nixon wanted to be closer to Washington, D.C. He wrote more books, mostly about world affairs. He visited world leaders. He spoke to groups, young and old. Slowly, his reputation improved. A few U.S. political leaders asked for Nixon's advice.

Nixon gives an interview in 1982. In the 1980s, Nixon became involved in public life again.

FROM LEFT: Pat and Dick Nixon, Nancy and Ronald Reagan, George and Barbara Bush, and Betty and Gerald Ford celebrate the opening of the Nixon Library and Birthplace.

In 1990, he opened the Richard Nixon Presidential Library and Birthplace in Yorba Linda, California. The site included the house where Nixon was born.

The Nixons also enjoyed the company of their four grandchildren. In 1993, Pat, once a heavy smoker, died of lung cancer. Within ten months, Nixon died of a stroke. They share a burial plot at the Nixon Library in Yorba Linda.

Richard Nixon was not an easy person to know. He didn't trust people. He saw almost everything as a battle. And he believed that only the tough survived to win and succeed. The public can read Nixon's private papers and tapes. They show a man who had a hard time just being himself—if he even knew who that was.

The Reverend Billy Graham speaks at Nixon's funeral on April 27, 1994.

TIMELINE

RICHARD M. NIXON WAS
BORN ON JANUARY 9,
1913, IN YORBA LINDA,
CALIFORNIA.

In the year . . .

1937   Dick graduated from Duke University Law School.   Age 24

1940   he married Pat Ryan.

1941   the United States enters World War II.

1942   the Nixons moved to Washington, D.C. Dick joined the U.S. Navy and served with the South Pacific Combat Air Transport Command (SCAT).   Age 29

1946   he won his first congressional campaign.

1950   he won his race for the U.S. Senate.   Age 37

1952   he ran as vice president with Dwight Eisenhower.

1956   he was re-elected.

1960   he lost to John F. Kennedy in the presidential election.   Age 47

1962   Dick lost the governor's election in California.

1968   he won his first presidential election.   Age 55

1972   he won his second term as U.S. president.

1974   he resigned from the presidency.

1990   he opened the Richard Nixon Presidential Library and Birthplace in Yorba Linda.

1993   Pat Nixon died.

1994   Richard Nixon died on April 22.   Age 81

2007   the National Archives took over the Nixon Library.

PATRICIA RYAN NIXON

Born in 1912, Patricia Ryan *(below)* grew up on a small farm near Whittier, California. By 1930, both her parents were dead. Pat kept herself and her brothers together. At the same time, she was an excellent student. She graduated from high school with top grades.

In 1931, she jumped at the offer to drive an older couple to the East Coast. She eventually lived in New York City. While there, she learned to dress with quiet style. She developed self-confidence. When she returned to California, she enrolled at the University of Southern California. She graduated in 1937. Her first job was as a teacher at Whittier Union High School. Soon afterward, she met Dick Nixon at the Community Players.

After Nixon's wartime service, Pat focused on making a home for him and raising their two daughters. A life in politics wasn't her first choice. But after Nixon decided on politics, she supported him completely from the sidelines. She weathered the rough times and enjoyed his successes. As First Lady, she traveled broadly and brought quiet formality to White House events. She encouraged Americans to volunteer to help others. After Watergate, she was happiest out of the spotlight. She died in 1993.

FURTHER READING

Burgan, Michael. *The Vietnam War.* **Portsmouth, NH: Heinemann, 2004.** This book gives a short history of the war.

Gaines, Ann Graham. *Richard M. Nixon.* **Mankato, MN: Child's World, 2001.** This books gives a general overview of Nixon's life.

Landau, Elaine. *The President's Work.* **Minneapolis: Lerner Publications, 2004.** This book covers the job of the president and how a president's choices affect the American people.

Otfinoski, Steve. *People at the Center of Watergate.* **Farmington Hills, MI: Blackbirch, 2005.** This book discusses the people who were involved in the Watergate scandal.

Schultz, Randy. *Richard M. Nixon.* **Berkeley Heights, NJ: Myreportlinks.com, 2003.** Internet links make this biography of Nixon stand out.

Thomas, William. *The Home Front in the Vietnam War.* **Strongsville, OH: World Almanac Library, 2005.** This book talks about what the American people were feeling and doing during the Vietnam War.

WEBSITES

Ben's Guide to U.S. Government
http://bensguide.gpo.gov/3-5 This website has lots of information about the documents and workings of the U.S. government. It also has games, activities, and links to other government websites for kids.

The Department of State
http://www.future.state.gov This website is for kids who, like Richard Nixon, are interested in foreign affairs. It has biographies, quizzes, and more.

The White House
http://www.whitehouse.gov/kids This site has background information and quizzes on all presidents and life at the White House.

SELECT BIBLIOGRAPHY

Ambrose, Stephen E. *Nixon.* 3 vols. New York: Simon and Schuster, 1987–1991.

Anson, Robert Sam. *Exile: The Unquiet Oblivion of Richard M. Nixon.* New York: Simon and Schuster, 1984.

Genovese, Michael A. *The Watergate Crisis.* Westport, CT: Greenwood Press, 1999.

Morris, Roger. *Richard Milhous Nixon: The Rise of an American Politician.* New York: Henry Holt, 1990.

Nixon, Richard. *In the Arena: A Memoir of Victory, Defeat, and Renewal.* New York: Simon and Schuster, 1990.

Small, Melvin. *The Presidency of Richard Nixon.* Lawrence: University Press of Kansas, 1999.

Wills, Garry. *Nixon Agonistes.* Boston: Mariner Books, 2002.

INDEX

Acknowledgments

For photographs and artwork: Nixon Presidential Library & Museum, National Archives, pp. 4, 29, 32, 40; © Steve Starr/CORBIS, p. 8; The Richard Nixon Library and Birthplace Foundation, pp. 9, 10, 11, 22, 43, 45; © Archive Photos/Hulton Archive/Getty Images, p. 12; © Fox Photos/Hulton Archive/Getty Images, p. 15; AP Photo, pp. 17, 18, 26, 38; © George Lacks/Time & Life Pictures/Getty Images, p. 19; © Bettmann/CORBIS, p. 20; AP Photo/The White House, p. 24; Dwight D. Eisenhower Presidential Library, p. 27; © Paul Schutzer/Time & Life Pictures/Getty Images, p. 28; Library of Congress, p. 31; The White House, p. 33; © Dirck Halstead/Liaison/Getty Images, p. 34; AP Photo/stf, p. 35; © Wally McNamee/CORBIS, p. 41; © Diana Walker/Time & Life Pictures/Getty Images, p. 42. Front Cover: The White House; Back Cover: The Richard Nixon Library and Birthplace Foundation.

For quoted material: p. 10, Roger Morris. *Richard Milhous Nixon: The Rise of an American Politician* (New York: Henry Holt, 1990), 66; p. 29, Melvin Small. *The Presidency of Richard Nixon* (Lawrence: University Press of Kansas, 1999), 22.